Clip and Copy Art
Holidays, Seasons and Events

by

Nancee McClure

Cover design by Tom Sjoerdsma and Jeff Van Kanegan

Copyright © Good Apple, Inc., 1989

ISBN No. 0-86653-486-5

Printing No. 98765

Good Apple, Inc.
Box 299
Carthage, IL 62321-0299

Table of Contents

GA1085

GA1085

Introduction

For centuries people have known that a good graphic image can enhance communication; hence the old saying, "A picture is worth 1000 words." This two-volume collection of fanciful drawings (over 600 copyright-free illustrations per volume) can be used to illustrate *your* messages in a light, humorous style.

The clip art is printed on one side only for your convenience. You can clip the illustrations directly from the book or make a photocopy of the artwork you plan to use. Apply adhesive to the back, using rubber cement, spray adhesive (such as 3-M SpraMount) or art wax. Place the illustration where you want it on your layout and press firmly. Sometimes the cut lines will photocopy as black lines. To solve this problem, make one photocopy and white out the cut lines and shadows. Use this as your master copy.

This volume of *Clip and Copy Art: Holidays, Seasons and Events* has been organized into sections by holidays from Halloween to the Fourth of July and includes illustrations for the four seasons, back-to-school, hobbies, recreation, money-making events, performances, organizations and much, much more. Use your clip art for:

Work Sheets	Games
Greeting Cards	Notices
Holiday Messages	Scrounge Lists
Party Announcements	Newsletters
Homework Papers	Fliers
Awards	Memos
Signs	Posters
Programs	Letters
Tests	Announcements
Advertisements	Collages
Invitations	Reports
Bulletins	School Newspapers
Brochures	Yearbooks
Booklets	Mailings
Handouts	Learning Centers

GA1085

Back to School

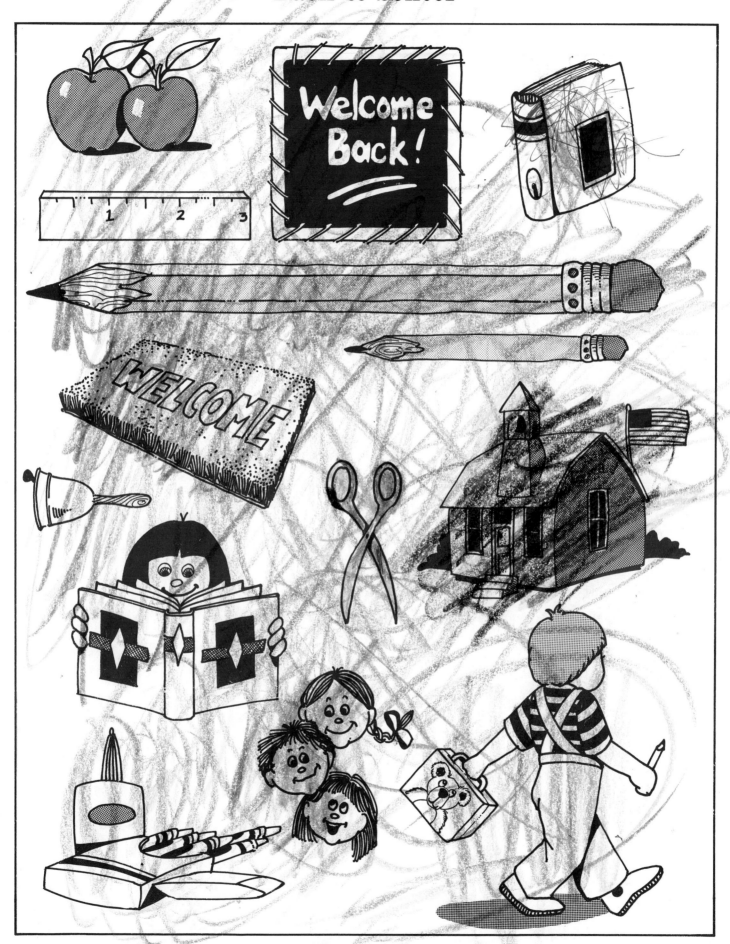

1

Back to School

3

GA1085

Teachers and Students

Halloween

7

GA1085

9

GA1085

Halloween Borders

11

GA1085

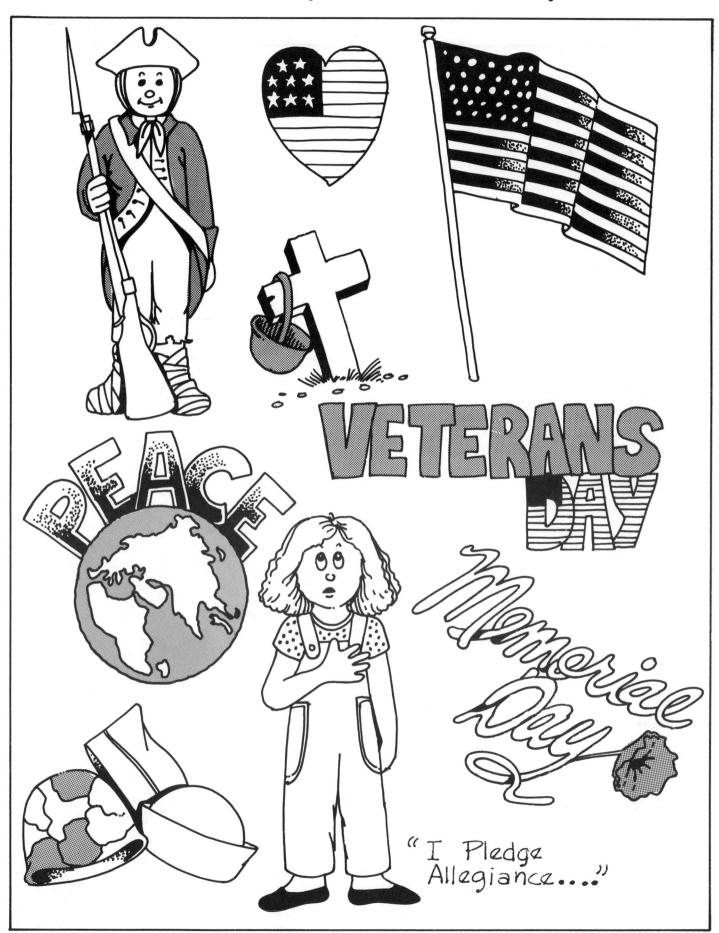

"I Pledge Allegiance....."

GA1085

Thanksgiving

15

Thanksgiving Borders

Christmas and Hanukkah

Jolly Holidays!

19

GA1085

21

GA1085

Holiday Season Borders

23

GA1085

25

27

Valentine's Day and St. Patrick's Day Borders

29

Easter

GA1085

Easter and Spring Borders

33

GA1085

35

GA1085

GA1085

Summer Vacation

VACATION!

CAMP
FUNZEE-WUNZEE

41

GA1085

Fall

43

GA1085

Winter

GA1085

GA1085

GA1085

GA1085

 GA1085

MY ROCK COLLECTION

HOBBIES ARE FUN

Circus and Carnivals

61

GA1085

Sports

YEA TEAM

GA1085

Be a Good Sport!

GO TEAM !!!

On Stage

Break a Leg!

Presenting:

ART SHOW

Craft Fair!

1st Prize

Clubs and Organizations

Art Club

Chess Club

Science Club

Math Club

CHORUS

Future Teachers

Computer Club

Future Farmers

GA1085

Banners and Frames

75

Banners and Frames

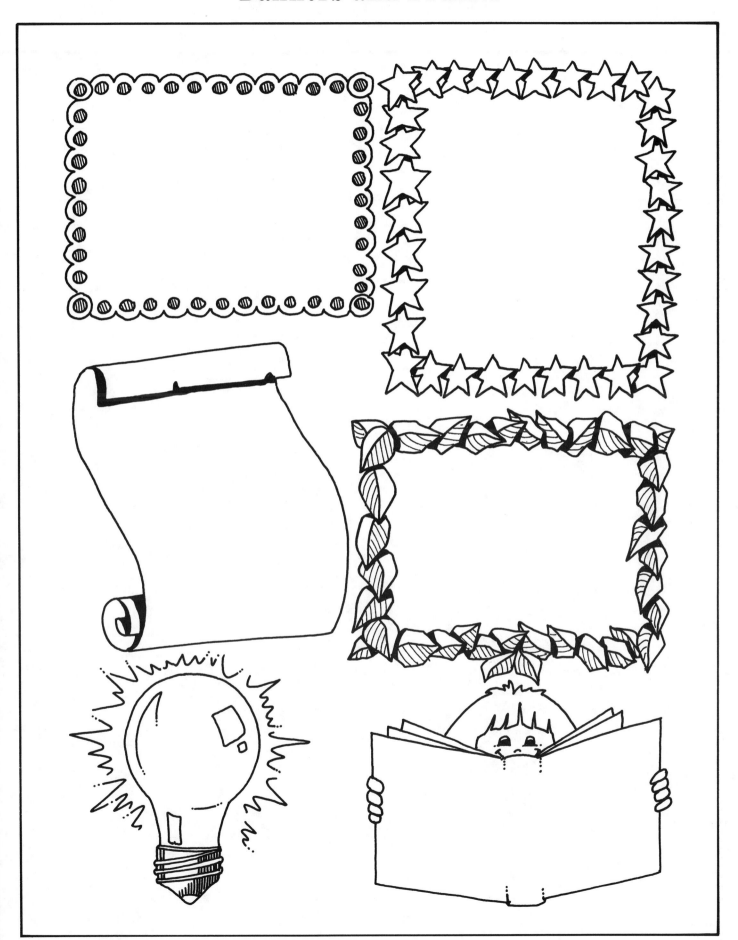

GA1085

GA1085

GA1085

Birthdays

GA1085

GA1085

89

Decorative Art

91

Decorative Art

93

GA1085

HEAR YE, HEAR YE

BREAKING NEWS

PITCH IN!

TODAY'S NEWS

FROM THE GRAPEVINE

Announcing

REMINDER

FOR SALE

Around Town

Good News...

GA1085

GA1085

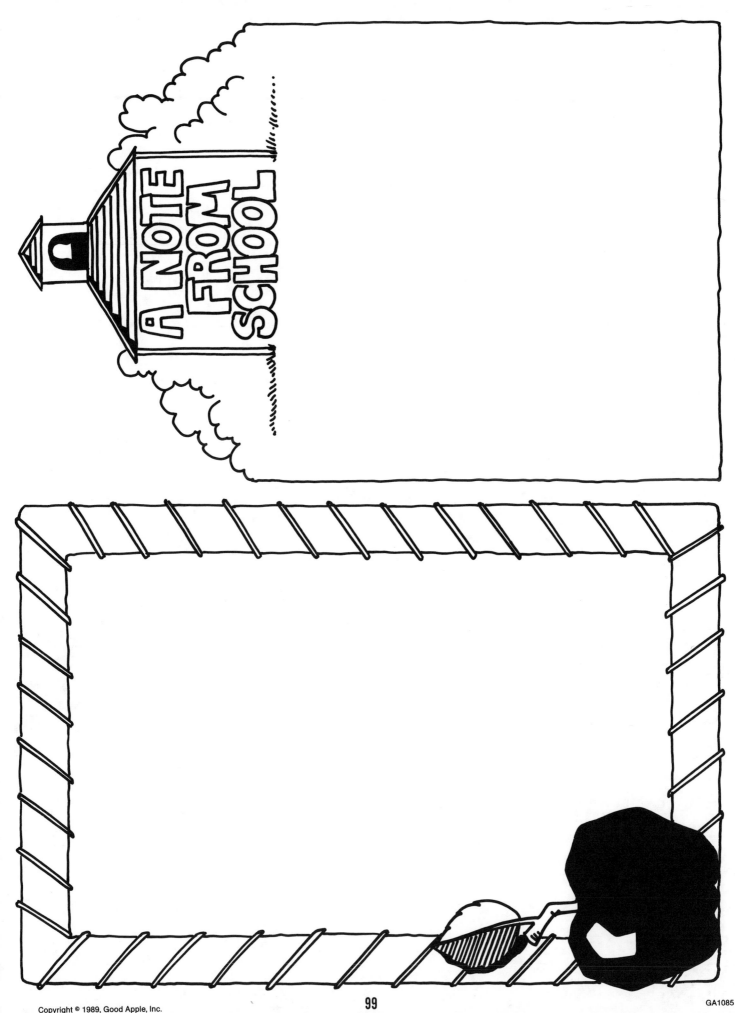

Month-at-a-Look

S	M	T	W	T	F	S

GA1085

Cut and paste these months and dates to individualize the calendar on page 101. You can also use the seasonal art on pages 1-51 to decorate each month.

January
February
March
April
May
June
July
August
September
October
November
December

1	2	3	4	5	6	7
8	9	10	11	12	13	14
15	16	17	18	19	20	21
22	23	24	25	26	27	28
29	30	31				

GA1085

Cut and Color Bookmarkers

GA1085

Greeting Card Art

I'm Sorry

107

Teacher Letterheads (Design your own letterheads, memos and note pads!)

Ask a Teacher!

A+

I'm Proud to be a Teacher!

A B C

Knowledge Is POWER!

109

GA1085

HOMECOMING

Sock Hop!

Class Reunion

MIXER

PEP RALLY

Prom

¡Bon Voyage!!

Announcements

GA1085

GA1085

GA1085

GA1085

121

GA1085

Dinosaurs

Spinosaurus

Pteranodon

Elasmosaurus

Triceratops

Brachiosaurus

Stegosaurus

Corythosaurus

GA1085

Arrows and Pointers

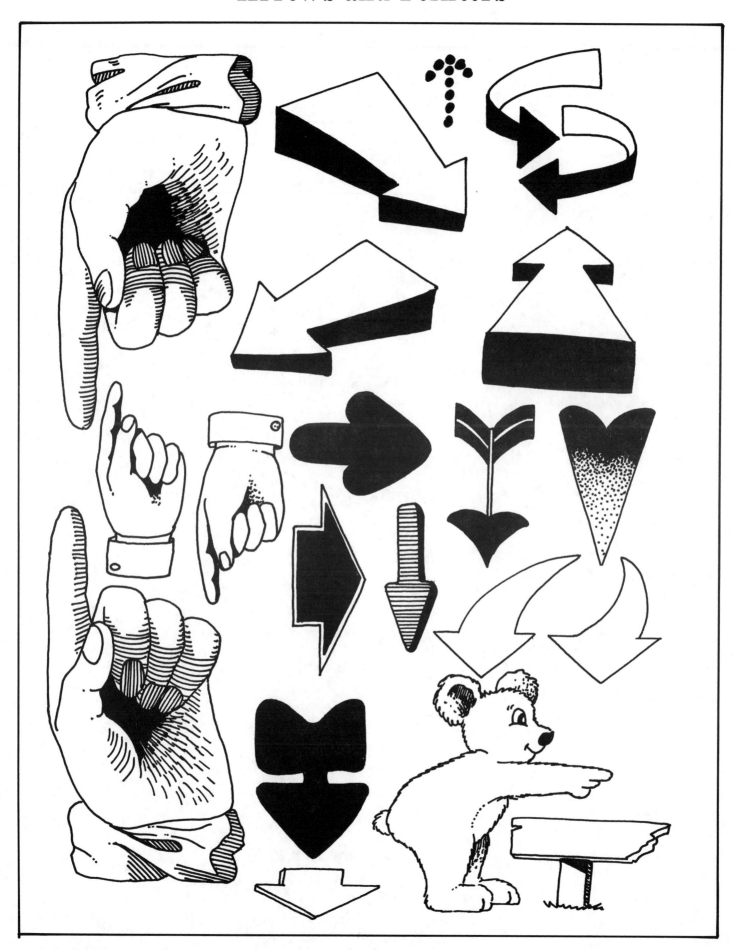

125

127

GA1085

Everyday Objects

129

GA1085

Emotions

131

CONGRATULATIONS, GRADUATE!

HATS OFF TO YOU!

GOOD LUCK IN HIGH SCHOOL!

GA1085

Miscellaneous Borders

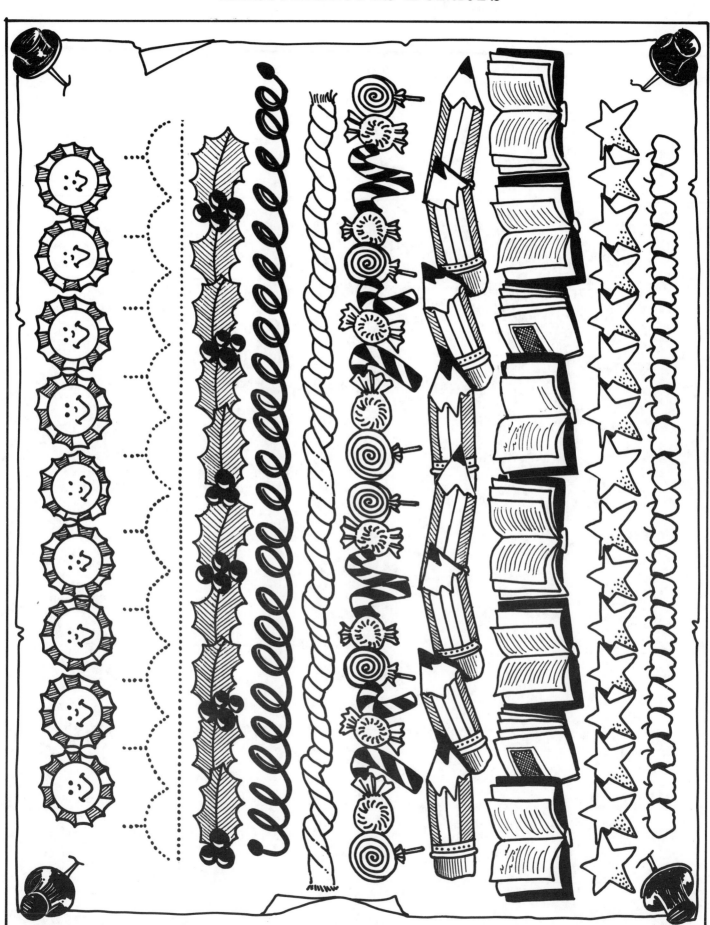

GA1085

Just for Fun

YIPPEE!

137

GA1085

You BRIGHTEN my DAY!

GOOD JOB!

THANK YOU!

YOU'RE THE GREATEST !!!

VERY IMPRESSIVE!

You're # 1

GA1085